THE PERPETUITY OF MADURO: RISE AND CONSOLIDATION OF POWER IN VENEZUELA

Moisés Rojas

CONTENTS

PROLOGUE

The recent history of Venezuela is marked by political and economic events that have captured global attention. From the rise of the Bolivarian movement led by Hugo Chávez to the consolidation of Nicolás Maduro's power, the country has undergone profound and controversial transformations. This book, "The Perpetuity of Maduro: Rise and Consolidation of Power in Venezuela," aims to offer a detailed and analytical look at the factors that have allowed Maduro to remain in power despite multiple crises and challenges.

In these pages, we will explore the historical context that preceded Maduro's rise to power, including the golden era of Venezuelan democracy and the factors that led to popular discontent. We will analyze how Chávez managed to capitalize on this discontent to implement the Bolivarian Revolution, and how Maduro, his designated successor, has used a combination of political, economic, and repressive tactics to consolidate his regime.

The methodology of this book is based on an extensive review of academic literature, reports from international organizations, interviews with experts, and testimonies from key actors in Venezuelan politics. Additionally, an effort has been made to include multiple perspectives, both for and against Maduro's government, to offer a balanced and comprehensive view of the situation.

We hope that this book will not only serve as a source of information for those interested in Venezuelan politics but also as a tool for reflection on the lessons that can be learned from the Venezuelan case in the broader context of Latin America and the world. The history of Venezuela under Maduro's regime is a complex narrative of power, resistance, and resilience, and it is crucial to understand it to anticipate future challenges and opportunities for democracy in the region.

PART I: HISTORICAL BACKGROUND

Chapter 1: Venezuela before Chávez

1. The Punto Fijo Pact Democracy (1958-1998)
   - **History of Democracy in Venezuela**: Since the

fall of Marcos Pérez Jiménez's dictatorship in 1958, Venezuela adopted a democratic system based on the Punto Fijo Pact, an agreement among the main political parties to ensure political stability and prevent coups.

- **The Punto Fijo Pact**: Details of the agreement between the parties Acción Democrática (AD), COPEI, and Unión Republicana Democrática (URD), and its impact on the country's political stability during the early decades of democracy.

- **Achievements and Failures of Democratic Governments**: Analysis of advances in education, health, and economic development, as well as issues of corruption, clientelism, and social inequality that contributed to disenchantment with traditional parties.

2. Economic and Social Crisis in the 80s and 90s

- **Dependence on Oil**: Explanation of how the Venezuelan economy became excessively dependent on oil, and how the drop in prices in the 80s led to a severe economic crisis.

- **The Caracazo**: A detailed analysis of the events of the Caracazo in 1989, a social uprising triggered by the increase in public transportation prices, which resulted in violent repression by the government of Carlos Andrés Pérez.

- **Disenchantment with Traditional Parties**: Exploration of how corruption, inefficiency, and unfulfilled promises by the AD and COPEI governments led to the rise of new political movements, including the Bolivarian Revolutionary Movement 200 (MBR-200) led by Hugo Chávez.

Chapter 2: The Era of Hugo Chávez

1. The Rise of Chávez
   - **Biography of Hugo Chávez**: His childhood in Sabaneta, his education at the Military Academy, and his career in the army.
   - **The 1992 Coup Attempt**: Details of the coup attempt led by Chávez against the government of Carlos Andrés Pérez, its failure, and the subsequent political consequences.
   - **The 1998 Electoral Campaign**: How Chávez capitalized on popular discontent with traditional parties, his anti-establishment rhetoric, and his promise of a "Bolivarian Revolution."

2. The Bolivarian Revolution
   - **Principles and Objectives**: Explanation of the Bolivarian ideology, based on the thoughts of Simón Bolívar, and the goals of social justice, inclusion, and national sovereignty.
   - **Political, Economic, and Social Reforms**: Description of the reforms implemented by Chávez, including the nationalization of key industries, wealth redistribution, and social programs known as "missions."
   - **1999 New Constitution**: Analysis of the drafting process of the new Constitution, its approval by referendum, and the significant changes it introduced to the government structure and citizens' rights.

3. Chávez's International Policy
   - **ALBA and Regional Alliances**: Creation of the

Bolivarian Alliance for the Peoples of Our America (ALBA) and its goals of integration and cooperation among Latin American countries.

- **Relations with the United States**: The growing confrontation with the United States, Chávez's anti-imperialist rhetoric, and the diplomatic and economic consequences.

- **Influence of Cuba**: Details of the close relationship between Venezuela and Cuba, including the exchange of oil for medical and security services, and Cuban influence on Venezuela's security and espionage policies.

PART II: THE RISE OF NICOLÁS MADURO

Chapter 3: From Bus Driver to Minister

1. Early Years and Political Career
    - **Biography of Nicolás Maduro**: His childhood in Caracas, his beginnings as a bus driver and union leader, and his entry into politics

through the Fifth Republic Movement.

- **Rise in Politics**: How Maduro became a close collaborator of Chávez, his role in founding the PSUV, and his election as a deputy and later president of the National Assembly.

2. Role in Chávez's Government

- **Minister of Foreign Affairs**: Analysis of Maduro's tenure as Foreign Minister, his role in Venezuela's foreign policy, and his relationships with international allies.

- **Closeness with Chávez**: How his personal and political relationship with Chávez strengthened Maduro's position within the government and the party.

- **Participation in the PSUV**: Details of his influence in the United Socialist Party of Venezuela and his role in the political strategy of Chavismo. Chapter 4: The Death of Chávez and the Succession

3. Chávez's Illness and Death

- **Chronology of the Illness**: Description of Chávez's cancer diagnosis, his treatments in Cuba, and the progression of his illness.

- **Political Impact**: The political and economic uncertainty generated by Chávez's illness and how the government managed the situation to maintain stability.

- **Death of Chávez**: Chávez's death in March 2013, the reactions within Venezuela and internationally, and the national mourning process.

4. Maduro's Election as Successor

- **Designation by Chávez**: Chávez's speech before

leaving for his final treatment in Cuba, in which he named Maduro as his successor.

- **2013 Electoral Campaign**: Maduro's electoral campaign against Henrique Capriles, the strategies used by both candidates, and the political tensions during the process.

- **Electoral Victory**: Maduro's narrow victory, the opposition's accusations of fraud, and the first measures taken by Maduro as president.

PART III: CONSOLIDATION OF POWER

Chapter 5: The Initial Difficulties

1. Economic Crisis
    - **Fall in Oil Prices**: Analysis of how the drop in oil prices in 2014 impacted the Venezuelan

economy, given the country's heavy reliance on oil exports.

- **Hyperinflation and Shortages**: Details of the hyperinflation phenomenon, the scarcity of basic goods, and how these crises affected the daily lives of Venezuelans.

- **Maduro's Economic Policies**: The economic measures adopted by Maduro, including price controls, currency devaluation, and their effectiveness or lack thereof.

2. Social Discontent and Protests

- **2014 Protests**: The causes of the student and popular protests in 2014, their development, and the government's repressive response.

- **Government Response**: Details of the repressive tactics used by the government, including the use of the National Guard and armed collectives.

- **Impact on Regime Stability**: How the protests and the government's response affected public perception of the regime and Maduro's political stability. Chapter 6: Political Control Strategies

3. The Use of the Constituent National Assembly

- **Creation and Justification**: The government's justification for convening a Constituent National Assembly in 2017, its election process, and the declared objectives.

- **Constituent Process**: How the drafting process of the new constitution was carried out, the lack of opposition participation, and international criticism.

- **Dissolution of the National Assembly**:

The dissolution of the opposition-controlled National Assembly and how the Constituent Assembly consolidated legislative power in the government's hands.

4. Manipulation of the Electoral System

- **Election Irregularities**: Examples of irregularities in presidential and regional elections, including voter registry manipulation and the lack of independent international observation.

- **Role of the National Electoral Council (CNE)**: The CNE's bias towards the government and its role in organizing and supervising elections.

- **Maduro's Re-election in 2018**: Details of the 2018 presidential elections, fraud accusations, and the responses from the opposition and the international community.

5. Reform and Control of the Armed Forces

- **Relationship with the Military Leadership**: How Maduro has secured the loyalty of the armed forces through the promotion of loyal officers and the granting of economic privileges.

- **Creation of the Bolivarian Militia**: Details on the creation of the Bolivarian Militia, its role in defending the regime, and its relationship with the regular armed forces.

- **Privileges and Benefits for Military Personnel**: The economic and social incentives granted to the military to maintain their support and prevent coup attempts.

PART IV: RESISTANCE AND OPPOSITION

Chapter 7: Protests and Social Movements

1. The Venezuelan Spring of 2014
    - **Origins of the Protests**: The underlying causes of the 2014 protests, including inflation, shortages of basic goods, and insecurity.

- **Development of the Protests**: How the protests were organized, the main actors involved, and key events during the demonstrations.
- **Government Response**: The repressive tactics used by the government, including the use of force, arbitrary detentions, and human rights violations.

2. Waves of Protests in 2017 and 2019
   - **2017 Protests**: Description of the massive protests in 2017, their organization, development, and the main events that marked these mobilizations.
   - **2019 Protests**: Details of the 2019 protests, including the political and economic context that triggered them, and the participation of various sectors of society.
   - **Impact of the Protests**: Evaluation of the impact of the protests on public perception of the government and the opposition, as well as on the stability of Maduro's regime. Chapter 8: Opposition Leadership

3. Fragmentation and Challenges of the Opposition
   - **Opposition Political Parties**: Analysis of the main opposition parties, their leaders, and their ideological and strategic differences.
   - **Lack of a Unified Strategy**: How the lack of a unified strategy has weakened the opposition and its ability to effectively confront the government.
   - **Failed Dialogue Attempts**: The efforts of dialogue between the government and the opposition, their failures, and the reasons behind the lack of concrete results.

4. Key Figures: Leopoldo López and Juan Guaidó
   - **Leopoldo López**: Biography and leadership of Leopoldo López, his role in the protests, and his imprisonment.

   - **Juan Guaidó**: Emergence of Juan Guaidó as an opposition leader in 2019, his proclamation as interim president, and his international recognition.

   - **International Impact**: How Guaidó's proclamation as interim president affected international policy towards Venezuela and the country's diplomatic relations.

PART V: INTERNATIONAL SUPPORT

Chapter 9: Allies and Enemies

5. Maduro's International Allies

   ◦ **Relationship with Russia and China:**

Analysis of economic and military relations with Russia and China, including loans, investments, and cooperation agreements.

- **Influence of Cuba**: Details on the relationship with Cuba, including cooperation in security and intelligence, and resource exchange.

- **Regional Alliances and ALBA**: The role of ALBA and other regional alliances in providing diplomatic and economic support to Maduro's government.

6. International Sanctions and Pressures

- **Economic and Political Sanctions**: Description of sanctions imposed by the United States, the European Union, and other countries, and their impact on the Venezuelan economy.

- **Role of the OAS and Other Organizations**: The participation of the Organization of American States (OAS) and other international organizations in denouncing human rights violations and applying diplomatic pressure on Maduro's government.

- **Government Response**: How Maduro's government has responded to international sanctions and pressures, including countermeasures and strategic alliances. Chapter 10: The Geopolitics of Power

7. Diplomatic Recognition and International Legitimacy

- **Battle for Recognition**: The struggle for diplomatic recognition between Maduro's government and interim president Juan Guaidó.

- **Role of Neutral and Mediating Countries**: The role of countries like Mexico, Norway, and Uruguay in mediation and negotiation attempts between the government and the opposition.

- **Influence of International Organizations**: The influence of organizations like the UN and the International Criminal Court on the political and human rights situation in Venezuela.

8. Interventions and Humanitarian Assistance

- **International Aid Efforts**: The international community's attempts to send humanitarian aid to Venezuela and the barriers imposed by Maduro's government.

- **Humanitarian Crisis**: Details on the humanitarian crisis in Venezuela, including the lack of food, medicine, and basic services, and the international response.

- ○ **Humanitarian Consequences and Responses**: Evaluation of the humanitarian crisis's consequences and the responses from international organizations and NGOs.

PART VI: ECONOMY AND SUSTAINABILITY OF THE REGIME

Chapter 11: The Deep Economic Crisis

1. Hyperinflation and Unemployment
    - **Causes of Hyperinflation**: Analysis of the economic policies that led to hyperinflation, including excessive public spending and the printing of unsupported money.

    - **Impact on the Population**: How hyperinflation has affected the purchasing power of Venezuelans, increasing poverty and inequality.

- **Government Measures**: The economic measures adopted by Maduro's government to control inflation, including the introduction of the petro and partial dollarization of the economy.

2. Shortage of Basic Products

- **Lack of Food and Medicine**: Description of the shortage of basic products, its causes, and how it has affected the daily lives of Venezuelans.

- **Black Market**: The emergence and growth of the black market as a response to shortages, and its impact on the economy and daily life.

- **Price Control Policies**: Analysis of the price control policies implemented by the government and their effectiveness or lack thereof. Chapter 12: Control of Natural Resources

3. Oil Exploitation

- **History of the Oil Industry**: Brief history of the oil industry in Venezuela, from its discovery to the nationalization of PDVSA.

- **Nationalization of PDVSA**: Details of the nationalization of the oil industry under Chávez and its impact on production and the economy.

- **Corruption and Mismanagement**: Examples of corruption and mismanagement in PDVSA under Maduro's government, and how they have contributed to the decline in oil production.

4. Mining and Other Industries

- **Orinoco Mining Arc**: Description of the Orinoco Mining Arc project, its objectives, and the controversies related to mining exploitation and environmental impact.
- **Illegal Mining**: The growth of illegal mining in Venezuela, its impact on the environment and indigenous communities.
- **Natural Resources and Management**: Other natural resources exploited in Venezuela and their management under Maduro's regime.

5. Corruption in Public Administration
- **Notorious Corruption Cases**: Examples of the most notorious corruption cases in Maduro's government, including the embezzlement of public funds and the involvement of high-ranking officials.
- **Impact on the Economy and Public Trust**: How corruption has affected the Venezuelan economy and public trust in the government and institutions.
- **Measures Against Corruption**: The measures adopted (or lack thereof) by the government to combat corruption and their effectiveness.

PART VII: FUTURE PERSPECTIVES

Chapter 13: Scenarios for Change

1. Paths to a Democratic Transition
    - **Possible Scenarios**: Analysis of possible scenarios for a democratic transition in Venezuela, including a negotiated settlement, a coup, or international intervention.

- **Role of the Opposition and International Community**: How the opposition and the international community can influence regime change, and the most effective strategies for achieving a peaceful transition.

- **National Reconciliation and Reconstruction**: The importance of national reconciliation and the reconstruction of social and institutional fabric in a post-Maduro scenario.

2. The Role of the Armed Forces

- **Influence of the Military**: The influence of the military on Venezuela's political future, and how they might act in different scenarios of change.

- **Internal Fractures**: Possible fractures within the armed forces and their impact on the regime's stability.

- **Guarantees for a Transition**: What guarantees can be offered to the military to facilitate a democratic transition and avoid internal conflict. Chapter 14: Lessons Learned

3. Lessons for Latin America and the World

- **Lessons from the Venezuelan Case**: The lessons that other countries can learn from the Venezuelan case in terms of populism, authoritarianism, and democratic resistance.

- **Importance of Strong Institutions**: The importance of having strong democratic institutions and an active civil society to prevent the rise of authoritarian regimes.

- **Role of the International Community**: The role that the international community can play in supporting democracy and human rights in crisis countries.

4. Final Reflections

- **Hope for Recovery**: Reflections on the hope for a future recovery for Venezuela, and the necessary steps to achieve it.

- **Resilience of the Venezuelan People**: The resilience and bravery of the Venezuelan people in their struggle for freedom and democracy.

- **Maduro's Legacy**: Evaluation of Maduro's legacy and its impact on Venezuela's history and future.

EPILOGUE

As we conclude this journey through the recent history of Venezuela and the regime of Nicolás Maduro, it is inevitable to reflect on the lasting impact of his government on the country and the region. Today's Venezuela is a testament to the deep political and social divisions that can arise in any nation, but also to the unbreakable resilience and hope of its people. Maduro has managed to perpetuate his power through a combination of tactics that include repression, electoral manipulation, and the consolidation of both internal and international alliances. However, history is not set in stone. The struggle for democracy and human rights continues, driven by a diverse opposition and an increasingly aware international community of the Venezuelan crisis. The lessons learned from the Venezuelan case are numerous and highly relevant for other countries facing similar challenges. The importance of strong democratic institutions, an active civil society, and a genuine commitment to the principles of justice and equity cannot be underestimated. Venezuela reminds us that democracy is fragile and must be constantly defended. Looking to the future, there are reasons for hope. History has shown that even the most authoritarian regimes can be challenged and eventually overcome. Venezuela's recovery will depend not only on a change in leadership but also on an inclusive process of reconciliation and reconstruction. The path will be long and difficult, but the determination of the Venezuelan people is a beacon of hope.

Ultimately, Nicolás Maduro's legacy will be judged by history. This book has attempted to offer a comprehensive and detailed view of the events and decisions that have marked his regime. We trust that readers, armed with this knowledge, will be able to contribute significantly to the debate on Venezuela's future and the strengthening of democracy throughout Latin America.

ABOUT THE AUTHOR

Moisés Enrique Rojas Zambrano

Moisés Rojas is a Venezuelan software engineer, born and raised in Venezuela. With a passion for technology and a deep connection to his homeland, Moisés has dedicated his career to software engineering, combining his technical knowledge with a unique perspective on Venezuela's political situation.

His personal and professional experiences in Venezuela until 2016, when he decided to move to Argentina, have provided him with a privileged and authentic view of the challenges and changes his country has faced. Through his book, Moisés shares his experiences and analysis, offering an intimate and detailed look at the complex political reality of Venezuela.

Currently, Moisés resides in Argentina, where he continues his work in the field of technology, while maintaining a firm commitment to spreading the truth and justice about the situation in his homeland.